Lamentations

*Not yet published as of this printing.

BIBLE STUDY COMMENTARY

Lamentations

DAN G. KENT

**Lamplighter
Books** Grand Rapids,
Michigan
Zondervan Publishing House

LAMENTATIONS: BIBLE STUDY COMMENTARY
Copyright © 1983 by The Zondervan Corporation
Grand Rapids, Michigan

Lamplighter Books are published by Zondervan
Publishing House, 1415 Lake Drive, S.E.,
Grand Rapids, Michigan 49506

Library of Congress Cataloging in Publication Data

Kent, Dan G.
    Lamentations: Bible study commentary.

    Bibliography: p. 63
    1. Bible. O.T. Lamentations—Commentaries. I. Title.
BS1535.3.K46   1983   224'.307   83-14522
ISBN 0-310-44011-4

Edited by Ed van der Maas

Printed in the United States of America

88 89 90 91 92 93 94 / CH / 10 9 8 7 6 5 4 3 2

To Barbara, of course, who—in the
stretches of her imagination—
has not yet realized how much
she has meant to me.

Lamentations

Introduction

They are five unusual little scrolls. The Hebrews grouped them together in their Bible and called them the *Megilloth* (Rolls).[1] They include the daring, rich Song of Songs and the simple, lovely Book of Ruth, as well as troubling Ecclesiastes and triumphant Esther. But the third scroll is unusual, too, and can hold its own with any other piece of literature because of its haunting beauty. We call it Lamentations.

A. Title

The little scroll originally had no title. The Hebrews called it by its first word, *Ekhah*, which is translated "How" (see also 2:1; 4:1). Since funeral dirges usually begin with this word, the Septuagint[2] called the little work *Dirges* and placed it after the Book of Jeremiah. This explains its position in our English Bible. The Vulgate added a subtitle identifying the book as the Lamentations of Jeremiah. We can still see this in many English versions today. (When we talk later about the authorship of Lamentations, we may wonder how many of us would ever think of associating it with the great Old Testament prophet if we had only the Hebrew

---

[1]The Hebrew Bible is divided into three sections: the Law (Genesis through Deuteronomy); the Prophets (Joshua through Kings, Isaiah, Jeremiah, Ezekiel, and the Minor Prophets); and the Writings (Psalms, Job, Proverbs, the *Megilloth*, Daniel, Ezra, Nehemiah, Chronicles).

[2]The Greek translation of the Old Testament. Much of the arrangement and naming of our Bible has been influenced by the Septuagint and the Vulgate, the Latin translation of the Bible.

text, without the influence of the later Greek and Latin versions).

B. Nature

Lamentations was written not long after the fall of Jerusalem to the Babylonians (587 B.C.). It describes and reflects on that fall in the most vivid of language. However, because of the complex structure of the five poems of the book (see below), it is likely that the bitterness of Nebuchadnezzar's terrible siege of the city had had time to pass. The poet could still remember everything that had happened, but he had also had time to begin to ask why it had happened and what it all meant. This book thus constitutes an important part of the nation's response to her downfall. It has well been said that the Book of Job relates suffering to a personal outlook, while Lamentations deals with suffering on a national scale and in historical terms.

The Old Testament itself is more than a book; it is an anthology of many different types of literature. One such type of literature is poetry, and one type of poetry is elegy.

The Old Testament elegy, Lamentations, is itself also a small anthology. It is a collection of five somewhat independent poems, each forming one chapter. It is intriguing that the first four of these five poems are acrostics: each stanza or strophe begins with the next consecutive letter of the Hebrew alphabet.[3] Since there are twenty-two consonants in Hebrew, there are also twenty-two verses in chapters 1, 2, and 4. (There is some slight variation of this pattern in chapters 2 and 4, where two of the later letters are reversed.) In other words, this book is a complex and elaborate composition.

Why did the author employ a mechanical device like the acrostic to convey such an intense expression of grief? Acrostics were often used as memory aids in ancient societies, but that seems unlikely in a collection of this type. The subject is too personal and intense to be merely an exercise in literary style along the line of "A is for apple; B is for ball; C is for cow." Also, the poems are so involved and so similar in con-

---

[3]See several psalms, including Psalm 119; the great hymn to womankind in Proverbs 31:10–31; and the first chapter of Nahum.

tent, it would be confusing to try to commit them to memory. We do know that the Jewish people later developed the superstition that the consonants of their alphabet were almost sacred or had magical powers. But that, too, is unlikely here.

Norman K. Gottwald[4] has suggested the most likely answer by pointing to the cathartic role of the acrostic. It was a means of achieving a complete cleansing through a total confession of sin, "a confession from A to Z," as we might say. (The Jewish Talmud speaks of keeping the law from *aleph* to *taw*).

Also, since the Hebrew people were given to ready outward expressions of emotion, a tightly structured acrostic form might have lent some control, some restraint, to what might otherwise have degenerated into an incoherent display of grief.

C. Authorship

The Book of Lamentations is anonymous, by which we mean that we do not know for sure who wrote it. The text of the book gives no author's name. But people then, like many today, were anxious to know the authors of anonymous Bible books. They preferred to associate such works with major figures.

Lamentations has traditionally been attributed to Jeremiah. The Septuagint and the Latin Vulgate translated by Jerome followed this Jewish tradition. So did the church fathers. The Septuagint even prefaces the book with these words: "And it came to pass, after Israel had been carried into captivity and Jerusalem had been laid waste, that Jeremiah sat weeping and lamented with his lamentation over Jerusalem and said . . . ." Some enterprising tour guides in Jerusalem will show you the very cave or grotto, near the Damascus Gate on the north side of the modern Old City, where, they will assure you, the aged prophet did his writing.

This tradition that Jeremiah authored Lamentations may have been based on a misreading of 2 Chronicles 35:25: "Jeremiah composed laments for Josiah, and to this day all the men and women singers commemorate Josiah in the laments.

---

[4]*Studies in the Book of Lamentations* (London: SCM Press, 1954), pp. 28–30.

These became a tradition in Israel and are written in the Laments." The King James Version translates the last word "lamentations." But what does the above verse say? Jeremiah composed lamentations for King Josiah. However, the Book of Lamentations is not about the death of Josiah in the year 609 B.C. (not even chap. 3, as some have suggested), but rather about the death of the city of Jerusalem in 587 B.C.

Let us examine briefly the major arguments for and against the authorship of Jeremiah. In support of Jeremiah are the following:

1. The authors of both books showed the same sensitive temper. Both were touchingly sympathetic with the nation in her sorrow. Both were ready to pour out the heart's emotions without restraint.

2. Both authors attributed the national calamity to the same cause: the sin of the people. Both held the religious leaders guilty. Both felt the people had depended on unreliable (foreign) allies.

3. Both authors used similar representations and figures, such as: the Virgin Daughter of Zion, irreparably breached (Lam. 1:15; Jer. 8:21); the writer's eyes flowing with tears (Lam. 1:16; 2:11; Jer. 9:1, 18); the feeling of being surrounded by terrors and fears; appeals for vengeance to the righteous Judge (Lam. 3:64–66; Jer. 11:20); the confidence that those who celebrated Judah's fall will become desolate in the same way (Lam. 4:21; Jer. 49:12). Also compare Lamentations 1:2 with Jeremiah 30:14.

4. Both books show striking similarities of expression.[5]

Against Jeremiah's authorship the following may be said:

1. The two authors wrote from different points of view.

a) Jeremiah said the Babylonians were carrying out the Lord's purposes in subduing Judah; Lamentations emphasizes the retribution due them. In fact, the writer of Lamentations anticipated that retribution and even called for it (1:21; 3:59–66).

b) "The law is no more, and her prophets no longer find visions from the LORD" (2:9) does not, to some, sound like

---

[5]For a list, see S. R. Driver, *An Introduction to the Literature of the Old Testament*, 9th ed. (Edinburgh: T. & T. Clark, 1913).

Jeremiah, but rather like someone who was not a prophet himself.

c) In 4:17 the speaker identifies himself with those who expected help from Egypt. Jeremiah never did (Jer. 2:18; 37:5–8).

d) The author of Lamentations had a higher regard for civil and religious leaders than Jeremiah showed. (See 1:6; 4:7; 5:12.) Lamentations 4:20 speaks in laudatory terms of the hapless Zedekiah, Judah's last king. Jeremiah called the king and his officials rotten figs, so bad they could not be eaten. He said they were abhorrent, an offense, a reproach, a byword, and an object of ridicule and cursing (Jer. 24:8–9).

e) Our poet had more concern for the official system of worship than Jeremiah ever showed (1:4, 19; 2:6, 9, 20; 4:16).

f) "Our fathers sinned and are no more, and we bear their punishment" (5:7). This verse is not easy to harmonize with the outlook of Jeremiah 31:29–30: "In those days people will no longer say, 'The fathers have eaten sour grapes, and the children's teeth are set on edge.' Instead, everyone will die for his own sin; whoever eats sour grapes—his own teeth will be set on edge."

2. The two books show differences in phraseology. Lamentations uses many words not found in Jeremiah. For example, *Adonai* (Lord) is used as a title for God, by itself, fourteen times in Lamentations 1–3. It is used only in combination with *Yahweh* (LORD) in Jeremiah. In many ways Lamentations is closer in style to some of the psalms, the later chapters of Isaiah, and Ezekiel than to Jeremiah.

3. Most important of all, the structure of Lamentations is too rigid for the Jeremiah we know. His style was so natural, varied, and unstructured, it was positively freewheeling by comparison.

People who have weighed the above arguments have reached different conclusions. Some have said the author was a disciple of Jeremiah (Baruch has been nominated), or was at least well acquainted with Jeremiah's writings and drew on Jeremiah's experiences and expressions.

Some have argued that the five poems had different authors. However, most now say that at least the first four came from the same heart and hand. And the current tendency is to think in terms of one author who, perhaps, wrote on different occasions. Some continue to argue for Jeremiah as the author. The arguments are inconclusive, and fortunately, the solution is not of primary importance.

Our poet, whoever he was, certainly lived at the same time as Jeremiah. He shared in the true prophetic spirit. He, too, was an eyewitness to Judah's death throes. He, too, probably remained in Judah during the Exile. Some have said chapters 3 and 5 were written later, but the tendency now is to date all five poems early, at least by 550 B.C.

Our poet was probably not a priest or a recognized prophet. He spoke of these groups like an outsider. Perhaps he was a civil leader, perhaps a member of the court of King Zedekiah, Judah's last ruler. Perhaps he was a military leader. If this were so, it would explain his reference in 4:18–20, which many take to mean that he joined Zedekiah in his flight from the city at the end of the siege (2 Kings 25:4–6).

Regardless of who he was, our poet was a man of deep spiritual perception. He was also a man of faith, who lived in a day that assailed faith. This book is a partial record of his spiritual struggle.

D. Use

These poems seem to be, in the main, private expressions of grief, but the exiles may have used them in their memorial ceremonies in Babylon to commemorate the fall of Jerusalem. Perhaps those who remained in Judah during the Exile gathered at the ruins of the temple for a regular memorial observance.

It is in line with the above suggestions that poems (and chapters) 1, 2, and 4 are called national funeral dirges and chapter 5 a communal lament. Chapter 3 is an individual lament (compare Psalms 7 and 22) with elements of thanksgiving and trust. The acrostic form would give the worshiping community a symbolic means of expressing full confession of sin and despair, plus a full expectation of the Lord's forgiveness and restoration.

After the Roman general Titus destroyed Jerusalem in A.D.

70 during the Zealot revolt, faithful Jews read Lamentations to help them remember the latest in a series of tragic days. Many churches use the book during Holy Week, in preparation for Easter, to help them meditate on the sufferings of Christ.

E. Message

Is it possible to continue to believe in the Lord in a world like ours, where things are going on like those we see happening all around us? People are wondering that today. Many seem to be answering the question in the negative. The circumstances seem to have made it impossible for them to believe in the Lord any longer.

It is an old, old problem. We know it is, because it is exactly the problem that lies behind Lamentations. This book is a part of the Hebrew people's attempt to preserve their faith in the Lord during the holocaust of the sixth century B.C.

For Further Study

1. In an Old Testament history or Old Testament survey read about the period from the death of Josiah (609 B.C.) through the first return from exile (538 B.C.).

2. Read the section on the authorship of Lamentations in an introduction to the Old Testament or a one-volume commentary. List the arguments for and against authorship by Jeremiah and compare them with the discussion above.

3. Use a secular history to make a study of the Babylonian Empire under Nebuchadnezzar.

Poem One

The Sorrowing City

Poem One

The Sorrowing City
(Lamentations 1:1–22)

In this funeral dirge the sorrowing city is personified, in typical Hebrew fashion. She is personified as a widow. She is bereft. She is weeping bitterly. She is not only alone (v. 1), she is utterly forsaken. She has been betrayed. She sits despised.

The first poem is made up of three-line strophes, each line consisting of two parts. The poem also follows the 3:2 or *qinah* rhythm, long called the dirge meter.[1] It is a remarkable vehicle for the expression of grief. And the poem is an acrostic: each of the twenty-two verses begins, in consecutive order, with the twenty-two consonants of the Hebrew alphabet.

A. Zion's Condition Described (1:1–11)

Even in English the poem has a depressing, sobering tone: "deserted," "widow," "slave." And those terms are all found in verse 1 alone.

The first eleven verses of the poem are written in the third person. They are a description of the condition of the forlorn city. Destitute Zion represents the fallen nation of Judah (see v. 3). She represents the Lord's people, referred to variously as "the city" (v. 1), "the Daughter of Zion" (v. 6), and "Jerusalem" (vv. 7–8).

Even the first word of the poem is important. The exclama-

---

[1]For a more detailed discussion, see R. K. Harrison, "Hebrew Poetry," *The Zondervan Pictorial Encyclopedia of the Bible*, 1975, Vol. III, pp. 80–81.

tion "How" is often used to introduce dirges like this one. We will see it again in 2:1 and 4:1. Isaiah and Jeremiah also used it (Isa. 1:21; Jer. 48:17).

"How" in verse 1 draws back the curtain to reveal the widowed city sitting—in the sense of living or existing—empty. She had been full of people. She had been a bustling commercial, political, and religious center. She had been great among the nations. She had been a princess among the provinces. But what a comedown! She has become empty and is now sentenced to forced labor.

Each of the three pairs of lines in verse 1 presents the after and the before. Each contrasts what Zion has become with what she once was. The last pair of lines reverses the order of the contrasting pictures (first before and then after) and thus sharpens the contrast.

No wonder the city is weeping, even in the night. No wonder the tears roll down her cheeks (v. 2). To make things worse, there is no one to comfort her. Either no one is around to do so, or no one who is around cares to do it. All her lovers and supposed friends have dealt treacherously with her. In fact, they have become her enemies.

The phrase "all her lovers" (v. 2) recalls the messages of Hosea and Jeremiah. The people had been so unfaithful to their covenant relationship with the Lord that the prophets describe them as spiritual adulterers. They had forsaken the Lord for other gods, other lovers, in the pattern of the Canaanite fertility religion. These "lovers" had not only turned out to be false; they had turned on Zion and become her foes.

Another possible understanding of "lovers" and "friends" (v. 2) would be that they represent the nations that allied themselves with Judah against the Babylonian overlord, nations like Egypt, Edom, Moab, and Ammon. They not only have not gone to her aid when she was attacked; they have allowed her to be defeated, or have even participated in her downfall. Yes, they have conducted themselves treacherously (v. 2 NASB).

The weight of the Lord's judgment on Judah is indeed heavy. The little kingdom has suffered exile and harsh servitude. Her people have been scattered among the nations. There is no respite from the tragedy. Her pursuers have overtaken her in the midst of her trouble (v. 3). In this verse the nation itself is personified as a woman; this illustration is apparently used interchangeably with the previous picture of the city of Jerusalem personified in this same way.

Verse 4 personifies even the roads that lead to and from the stricken city, and pictures them as also mourning over Zion's sad condition. Why, no one is traveling them as they normally did. No pilgrims are making their way to Jerusalem for any of the festivals, the religious holidays. Her gates are unused and the squares or plazas just inside those gates are deserted. Temple worship is no more. The city herself suffers bitterly (NASB mg.).

"Zion" is strictly only a part of the city of Jerusalem. In Old Testament times the name referred to the temple mount. However, in this book and elsewhere it is used to represent the city as a whole.

Because of the city's emptiness, the priests groan. The maidens who had some role in the religious system are grief-stricken also. The verbs in verse 4 are participles; they express long, continuing action. This serves to intensify the picture of the misery of the situation.

Zion's fortunes and the fortunes of her foes must have seemed to be on a seesaw. As hers declined, theirs rose. Therefore verse 5 says her adversaries have become her masters. Her enemies are prospering. Her condition is further described in terms of her children having been taken away as captives before these adversaries.

In verse 5 we also come to one of the great theological insights of this book: "The LORD has brought her grief because of her many sins." This little book not only paints vivid pictures of the sorrows of the city; it also interprets those sorrows. It tells why it all happened. The Lord has not lost His power. He has not become deaf to their cries or blind to their situation. He has not been defeated by any foreign god. In fact, He Himself has brought the tragedy about—but He only did it because He had to. The people themselves forced Him to send judgment on their repeated sin. As He often did, He used foreign peoples as His instruments of punishment.

This is why all Zion's majesty has departed. This is why her princes have become like deer who cannot find pasture (contrast Ps. 23:2, 5). This is why they have had to flee, weak and defenseless, before their pursuers (v. 6). Judah's last king, Zedekiah, tried to escape from Jerusalem just before the city fell to Nebuchadnezzar, but he and his advisers were captured (2 Kings 25:4–6).

Verse 7 makes the touching picture even more poignant. In the time of her affliction and hopelessness the widow Jerusalem remembers. When her people fell into the hand of the adversary, when no one helped her, when her adversaries mocked her in her ruin, she recalled how splendid her former life had been. This brings to mind the old proverb about missing the water when the well runs dry.

Notice that verse 7 is made up of more lines than is normal in the verses of this chapter. Many scholars think one or another was added later. Some say one line preserves a variant reading that was somehow added to the passage. The unexpected change of pattern serves to call attention to the poignancy of the portrait.

Verse 8 returns to the spiritual interpretation of the tragedy of Jerusalem's destruction. She has greatly sinned. Literally, she "has sinned a sin." The Hebrew language had little in the way of comparative or superlative constructions, so the Hebrew people repeated or pluralized something when they wanted to emphasize it.

The Holy City herself has become unclean. Because of this unholy transformation, those who at one time honored her have come to despise her. She has been shamed before them. They have seen her nakedness. She can only groan and turn away.

The first phrase of verse 9 simply continues the personification characteristic of the entire poem. It means that the city is filthy[2] because of sin. Then we have a more spiritual interpretation of the city's situation. She did not take the long look. She did not consider the ultimate consequences of what she

---

[2]The reference is apparently to the stain of menstrual blood.

was doing. That is why she has fallen in such an astonishing way. That is why she has found no comforter.

A new idea appears at the end of verse 9. It will be elaborated considerably in the last half of the chapter. The final pair of lines in verse 9 are a fragment of a prayer to the Lord. This is remarkable, since the only reference to the Lord up to this point has been as the Judge of the people's sinfulness. But the people have retained a relationship with Him. He had to judge them, but He is still their God.

Therefore the city prays, "Look, O LORD, on my affliction." The implication is that when the Lord becomes aware of someone's need, He moves to meet it. The brief prayer also asks the Lord to see how the enemy has magnified himself in triumph.

The third-person description resumes in verse 10. Like fingerprints soiling delicate magnolia blossoms, the adversary has laid hostile hands on all her precious things (see vv. 7, 11). The heathen nations have entered her very sanctuary. Why, those pagan peoples were not allowed to even enter the congregation of the Lord's people without a personal faith commitment to Him. And now they have violated His very sanctuary and carried off its sacred treasures.

The first section of the poem concludes with a summary description of the hardship caused by the defeat and the suffering that inevitably followed it. The famine that was such a tragic part of Nebuchadnezzar's siege of Jerusalem has continued: hungry people are forced to roam around seeking after food. They have to give up whatever they hold dear in order to sustain their lives.

Then, at the very end of the section, there is a second brief prayer. It is quite similar to the one at the end of verse 9: "Look, O LORD, and consider." It is a prayer to the Lord to look on one who is in such need and is so despised.

B. Zion's Lament Expressed (1:12–22)

At this midpoint in the poem the scene shifts. The city herself begins to express her grief. The torrent of her lamentation that pours forth is almost overwhelming. It is even more touching than the previous description has been.

Grief and lamentation, yes. Notice, however, that there is no note of resentment here. She frankly admits that the tragedy that has come is her own fault. She has been rebellious. She has forced the Lord to act and has suffered as a consequence.

Verse 12 is one of the most familiar and penetrating laments in all of Scripture. It has been used in cantatas to express the pain and isolation of Christ on the cross. It is a general appeal for pity. It is an appeal for someone, anyone, to see and sympathize. Don't ignore me, is the plea. See, please see, and care (see v. 18; 2:15).

It is human nature to always think about ourselves in the superlative degree. Our problems are more serious than anyone else's. Our day is more wicked than any previous era. Our needs are greater than anyone else's.

In this case, however, sorrowing Zion definitely has a point. Her agony is great. It is almost without parallel or comparison. And the worst thing of all is this: it did not have to happen. The Lord had to cruelly punish (see NEB) His people because of their sin (v. 12).

From His throne on high the Lord has sent the fire that burned itself right down inside her. It has descended on her and overwhelmed her (see NASB mg.). Then the metaphors change. He has spread out a net for her and has caught her in it (The prophets used this illustration frequently, Hos. 7:12; Ezek. 12:13). He has turned her completely around. He has made her desolate and weak, stunned, even faint [or sick, NASB mg.] all the day long. As a result she is desolate, miserable (v. 13).

Zion laments that she is suffering under a yoke; however, the truth of the matter is that the hand of the Lord Himself has constructed this yoke. It is a yoke made up of her transgressions. These transgressions, these rebellious or mutinous acts, have fallen as a heavy burden on her own neck. In this way the Lord has made her strength waver. She is ready to stumble under the load. He has given her into the hands of those who are too strong for her (v. 14).

In His judgment the Lord has dealt with all her strong men by assembling superior enemy forces. He has finally called her to account. Her young men have fallen in futile battle. He has trodden as in a wine press the "Virgin Daughter of Judah" (v. 15).

Some think that the picture in verse 15 is of the Lord's judgment on Judah as a sacrificial feast. Some of the prophets do indeed present such an unusual picture (Isa. 34:6; Zeph. 1:7–8; Jer. 46:10). The final sentence of the verse seems to say that the wine for the feast was the blood squeezed out of the bodies of those who fell in battle.

Once again we say, no wonder she weeps as she does. No wonder her eyes flow with the water of tears. No wonder there are no comforter and no comfort. No wonder there is no restorer. As she has already lamented, her children are desolate and the enemy victorious (v. 16).

In the first half of the poem we found brief fragments of prayer interspersed in the narrative description (vv. 9, 11). In that same fashion we find here a brief descriptive section appearing like a parenthesis in the lament: verse 17. Zion stretches or spreads out her hands, groping about her in her grief, but it is no use; there is no one to comfort her. The reason is that the Lord has willed otherwise. He has commanded that the ones around fallen Judah shall be opposed to her, and that Jerusalem herself shall be an unclean thing among them. The "neighbors" of this verse are evidently the "lovers," "friends," and "allies" of verses 2 and 19.

"The Lord is right," the first phrase of verse 18 might be translated. He is righteous and what He has done is right. The fault is all on my side, the stricken city confesses, not on His. "I rebelled against his command." And once again she calls out to all peoples to hear her cry and observe her suffering (see v. 12). Her young women and young men—in other words, the nation's future—have all been taken away as captives. It is almost as if she has acknowledged the justice of her punishment and then turns around to protest its severity. To paraphrase this passage (which reminds us of Job's complaint), "Sure, I have sinned, but have I sinned *this badly?*" It is a strong confession, but it appears in a melancholy setting.

The confession continues in verse 19. She admits that she has called to her lovers (supposed allies like Egypt), but they have deceived her. Her leaders both spiritual and civic have perished with the fall of the city. They fell even as they were in the process of seeking food to sustain themselves.

In verse 20 the confession turns into prayer (see vv. 9, 11). Once again it is a prayer to the Lord to see. Lord, see what distress I am in. See how troubled I am, both inside and out. See how my insides (the seat of emotion to the Hebrews) are churning (see NASB mg.). My heart (the seat of intelligence and will) is turned over within me. Yes, I have been rebellious in the extreme. As a result, the sword has killed and death (or pestilence) reigns inside the houses.

People know that I groan in my pain, her lament continues, but there is no one to comfort me. All my enemies have heard about the evil that has befallen me, but they do not offer comfort. Instead they are glad. And the last part of verse 21 becomes a cry to the Lord for vengeance on these enemies who have brought about such destruction: make them like me. Make their situation like my own, as you have promised to do. Pay them back in their own coin. Deal with them as you have dealt with me (v. 22).

In all of the imprecations like this one, throughout the Old Testament, there is a strong note of personal vengeance. However, there is also the confidence that the Lord is truly the Lord of all the world. That means that no evildoer will go unpunished. If the Lord so punished His own people, He will judge others also. And there is the implied recognition in the prayer that the God who punished is still the only hope.

For Further Study

1. Begin a "Before/After" list enumerating the contrasting characteristics of Jerusalem preceding and subsequent to the destruction.

2. Use a concordance to make a study of the term "Zion." How does it relate to the name "Jerusalem"?

3. Read the Book of Hosea to make a study of the idea of "lovers" as it relates to idolatry, immorality, and foreign alliances.

4. Begin a list of passages indicating why the Lord had let such terrible things happen to the people.

5. Begin a list of prayers prayed throughout the book.

6. Begin a list describing the nature, actions, and words of the enemies.

7. Begin a list of the references to animals in this book.

Poem Two

Focusing on the Lord

Poem Two

Focusing on the Lord
(Lamentations 2:1–22)

We see many elements in this poem similar to the previous one. As before, the people's suffering is described. Again the onlookers show contempt. Again the dirge ends in a prayer placed in the mouth of the city (vv. 20–22). Again the tragedy is seen as judgment on sin. Again the purpose of the Lord is recognized.

This time, however, the foes rejoice more vividly and the lamentation as a whole is less formal and more detailed. This time the poet is the speaker throughout (see 1:1–11). And this time the focus is definitely on the Lord. God Himself is the subject of half of the sentences.

This second elegy is also an acrostic. Each verse of three pairs of lines begins with a consecutive Hebrew consonant. However, as also is the case in chapters 3 and 4, the sixteenth and seventeenth letters are reversed.

A. The Result of the Lord's Anger (2:1–10)

The author of these poems was definitely an eyewitness to Jerusalem's fall. His description is too specific and his details too precise for us to think otherwise.

Once again the poem begins with the exclamation "How." The Lord has disgraced the Daughter of Zion by covering her with the cloud of His anger (or contempt, see NIV mg.). He has taken the glory or splendor (perhaps the temple or the city itself) and, as it were, cast it from heaven down to earth like a falling star. He has refused to remember His footstool (again

the city, or more probably the temple) in the day of His anger
(v. 1). (The apparent reference in verse 1 to the fall of Babylon
in Isaiah 14:12–20 hints that Judah has been treated as if she
were a heathen nation.)

The Lord has swallowed up His people Jacob. He has consumed them, destroying them completely, verse 2 says. He
did not spare their dwellings. In His wrath He has torn down
their strongholds. He has leveled them; he has brought them
down to the ground. He has profaned the kingdom and its
leaders.

Notice the repetition of the ideas of anger (v. 1), wrath (vv.
2, 4), and fierce anger (vv. 3, 6) in these verses. They help us
to look at an idea of judgment from the Lord's perspective.
This is why He acted savagely and without pity. This is why
He cut off all the strength or power (Heb.: horn) of his people
(see also v. 17). He has burned up Jacob like a flaming, con-
suming fire (v. 3). He weakened her and then He withheld
His help. He withdrew His hand (see Ps. 74:11) and allowed
the enemy to dominate. He even took the offensive against
His own, as Jeremiah had once predicted.

The Lord bent His bow as the enemy bent his. He set His
right hand against Jerusalem even as the enemy did. He slew
all the notable people in her (her treasured people). He
poured out His wrath like a fire on her "tent" (v. 4). The latter
may refer to the temple but more probably indicates the
houses of the people. The first five verses of the chapter seem
to refer more to the land and the people, while references to
the Temple are more obvious in verses 6–7.

Yes, the Lord has become like an enemy. He has swallowed
up Judah. He has swallowed (see also vv. 8, 16) her modest
palaces and destroyed her supposed strongholds. (No strongholds are strong against Him.) In the process he has multi-
plied for the Daughter of Judah mourning and lamentation
(v. 5). The Hebrew words for these last two terms are not only
synonymous, they are also alliterative. This repetition of ini-
tial sound helps reinforce the poignant picture. The first one
speaks of sorrow or grief; the latter has the idea of moaning.

In our contemporary slang we would say the Lord "laid her
out." He destroyed the supposedly Holy Place, the temple, as

if it were a temporary hut out in the field or garden. His fierce anger against the people's sin caused Him to spurn both civil and religious leaders. The shock, the trauma was so great, the people of Zion completely forgot their feasts and sabbath observances (v. 6). How could they observe them? Yes, they were commanded to do so in the Law, but now there is no place for them and no opportunity. Thus the Lord has abolished temple, priest, king, and worship.

When He disowned the altar He had commanded to be built, that was named by His name, that was dedicated to His worship, where sinful man came to find reconciliation with a holy God—when the Lord rejected that altar and its sanctuary, when He handed the walls of the palace-temple complex over to the enemies, then those enemies raised a triumphant shout. They did so in the very house of the Lord. They did so "as on the day of an appointed feast" (v. 7). What could be more heartrending than that? Zion has forgotten her appointed feasts; her shouts of joy on those days have been silenced. Yet there is a shout in the sacred area, not of joy but of victory, the shout of the arrogant, triumphant enemy.

When the Lord determined to tear down His wall of protection around the city of Jerusalem, He did so. He did it thoroughly. He did such a thorough job of destruction that even the ramparts and walls are said to have uttered laments as they wasted away. All this because He put the plumb line to the city to discover its defects by measuring it against His perfect standard (v. 8; see Amos 7:7–9).

The gates of an ancient city were among the strongest parts of its fortifications. This made it all the more significant that the poet describes Jerusalem's gates as sunk down into the ground, their bars broken. Her political leaders are in exile. Even the prophets no longer receive visions from the Lord (see v. 14). No wonder "the law is no more" (v. 9); no one is left to uphold it or teach it to the people.[1] Yes, the Lord has utterly forsaken them.

The conclusion of all the Lord's destroying activity is that

[1]Law, in the Old Testament, has the broad meaning of "teaching" or "instruction."

the elders (usually the heads of the families) are sitting, in helpless silence, on the ground. They have dressed in sackcloth and have sprinkled dust on their heads, the traditional Hebrew indications of mourning and repentance. The young women of the city have also bowed their heads to the ground in grief (v. 10). The local leaders have no duties to perform, nor can they do anything about the nation's sad plight.

B. The Agony of the Afflicted (2:11–17)

There is a shift between verses 10 and 11. It is an obvious shift in speaker and a less obvious shift in subject matter. The poet begins to express himself in the first person, bewailing the city's destruction and her pain.

Verse 11 is one of those verses that makes many students of the Old Testament think of Jeremiah (see Jer. 9:1). The poet has "cried his eyes out," as we say. His extensive weeping indicates the turmoil going on within. His heart is "poured out on the ground" along with many tears.

There is every reason to weep. The people have been destroyed (notice how this verb is repeated in this chapter). The few youngsters who remain are lying faint (probably from starvation) in the city streets (or squares; v. 11; see also vv. 19–21; 4:4, 10). This is the opening scene in a lengthy and detailed description of the people's suffering during the long siege of the city.

The plea of the children is recorded in verse 12. You can almost hear them whine, weakly but persistently, "Mamma, I'm hungry. I want a piece of bread. I want something to drink." "Bread [literally, grain] and wine" in this verse indicate normal foodstuffs. Even as they speak the youngsters fall over in a faint, like men falling wounded on the battlefield. Their little lives slip away as they lie in the very arms of their grieving mothers.

One of the overriding notes in this section is that of helplessness in the face of unprecedented and unique anguish. In verse 13 we see helplessness of expression. The poet despairs of being able to speak any effective word of comfort or cheer, or to offer any appropriate description. The wound of the nation is as deep as the sea (literally "great as the sea";

some take this to refer to the expanse of the sea, see RSV). It is completely beyond cure. Consequently, he is unable to help them understand or cope with their catastrophe.

One reason the avoidable tragedy was not avoided was the activity of popular prophets with false, worthless visions (see Ezek. 22:28). The oracles (messages) they delivered to the people were misleading, in part because they did not expose the people's sin, warn them of the fast-approaching doom (v. 14), or call them back to their covenant responsibilities under God. They kept on preaching what the people wanted to hear and assuring them that everything was going to be all right. And the people believed them.

The next two verses then speak of passers-by and enemies, two groups not necessarily mutually exclusive. Because of what the prophets did not do and because of what the Lord did, passers-by clap their hands in shock and amazement. They scoff. They shake their heads. They ask each other: "Is this the city that was called the perfection of beauty, the joy of the whole earth?" (v. 15). Why, it can't be!

In the case of the enemies (v. 16) this is adding insult to injury. Their mouths are opened wide in their braggadocio and their derision. They scoff. They gnash their teeth. They gloat over their victory and their victim's misfortune. And of course, they claim all the credit for themselves. It is the day they have always waited for; they have finally lived to see it. Jerusalem has become the laughingstock of the nations.

Some commentators feel there is an implied charge in these verses that the Lord does not see the plight of the people nor respond to their cry of need. Whether that is true or not, it is true that what happened is repeatedly attributed to the Lord. What took place, He did. It took place because He purposed for it to take place, and he carried out His purpose. Of course, He had no other recourse. This was only the fulfilling of His word that He had spoken through the Law and through His spokesmen, the prophets. He had spoken often and over a long period of time (v. 17).

Thus it became necessary for Him to overthrow His people without pity, which also involved exalting the strength (literally, horn) of the foes to the point that they would be able to gloat (v. 17). S. R. Driver spoke of the foes' "malicious triumph."

C. The Plea for Relief (2:18–22)

Now we have yet another shift in the pattern of the poem. This one takes us through the rest of the chapter. Verses 18–19 appeal to the people to cry out to the Lord. Later verses embody actual prayers for help.

As verse 18 says, the hearts of the people are already crying out to the Lord. "Prayer is the soul's sincere desire,/ Unuttered or expressed," as the old hymn says. The idea here is that the very tears, flowing continually like a river, constitute an appeal to the Lord. The verse urges the wall of Jerusalem to weep without relief and without rest (see v. 8). This means that, even though the destruction came from the Lord and was according to His plan, there is no hope for relief from any other source. The poet pleads with the city to turn to Him.

Her only recourse is to cry out in the night. She should do so throughout the three watches of the night.[2] She should pour her heart out like water in His presence. She should lift up prayerful hands to Him (v. 19).

In the last part of verse 19 we come to the reason the poet urges such unceasing, earnest prayer: it is for the sake of the children mentioned in verses 11–12. Pray for their lives, he says. They are dying from hunger at the corner of every street. Surely the Lord will respond to a situation like that.

Now comes the actual prayer the city prayed. It begins in a way that reminds us of 1:9, 11, 20: "Lord, look at my need; see my condition. Has there ever been anything like it?" And we modern readers begin to agree with this sentiment when we read about priest and prophet being killed in the sanctuary itself, and women eating their own beloved children (v. 20; see 4:10 and Jer. 19:9).

---

[2]In the Old Testament, the night was divided into three watches. The first watch was from sunset to 10 P.M., the second from 10 P.M. until 2 A.M., and the third or morning watch from 2 A.M. until sunrise. The phrase in verse 19 literally reads "at the head of the watches" and probably should be understood in the sense of "as each watch of the night begins," i.e., "throughout the night."

Prayer seems often to be a matter of reporting to the Lord, not to provide Him with information, but to indicate that we are aware of the situation and want Him to respond. The prayer in verse 21 describes the young and old lying dead together in the dust of the streets, with an entire generation of young men and women having been killed by the Chaldean (Babylonian) sword. An even more basic truth, however, is that the Lord has killed those who have been slain. Again the book repeats the conviction that He has had to act without pity.

The conclusion of the brief prayer is both beautiful and hauntingly poignant: Lord, in the same way that You used to summon Your people to the feast days, so you marshaled against me terrors on every side (see Jer. 6:25; 20:10). No one was able to survive the day of Your anger. "Those I cared for and reared, my enemy has destroyed" (v. 22). And so the poem ends without the prayer for vengeance we see at the end of chapters 1 and 3.

For Further Study

1. Check some major commentaries with regard to their identification of the Lord's footstool in 2:1 and "the tent" in 2:4.

2. Lamentations says that the Lord had become like an enemy to His people. In what sense could that be true today?

3. Use a concordance to make a study of some of the broader uses of "law" (teaching or instruction) as suggested above.

4. What lessons can we learn from the fact that this book indicts the religious leaders (prophets and priests) for their part in the terrible judgment on the city?

Poem Three

Personal Suffering and Hope

Poem Three

Personal Suffering and Hope
(Lamentations 3:1–66)

We notice immediately a change of pattern in the third poem. It, too, is an acrostic. However, in this case three two-part lines each begin with the same Hebrew letter. This accounts for the fact that there are three times as many verses in this chapter, but that the verses are much shorter. In some ways this is the most characteristic of the five poems in the book. It is certainly the most profound and personal.

At times the poet speaks for himself, but most often he speaks for the people. He speaks as if the sufferings of the people are his own personal experience. Also notice the repeated individual references in verses 1, 27, 35, 39. However, the lament is obviously that of the whole group in verses 40–47, and all of it was later used in group worship.

A. A Personal Experience of God's Wrath (3:1–18)

The opening verse of the third dirge says, "I am the man who has seen affliction." Once again the source of the affliction is the rod of the wrath of the Lord (see Isa. 10:5). The poet himself has undergone the worst of the Lord's judgment. This fact will make the expressions of confidence later in the chapter that much more meaningful.

Look at what the Lord has done to me, the poet laments in verses 1–16. He has driven me away from Him. He has made me walk in darkness rather than light (v. 2). He has made me dwell in darkness like those long dead (v. 6; see Ps. 143:3). I am as good as dead myself. He has turned His hand against

me, one of His covenant people. He has done so repeatedly.
He has done it "all day long" (v. 3).

Look at my outward appearance and see the evidences of
the rod of the Lord's wrath. (Some people think the reference
is to a specific illness.) He has made my skin and flesh old. He
has broken my bones (v. 4). He has fenced me round about
with bitterness (literally, gall) and hardship (v. 5). He has put
such a wall around me that I cannot escape; He has weighed
me down with chains (v. 7). He has barred my way with
blocks of stone; He has made my paths so crooked (v. 9) that
they lead to destruction rather than to help. Even when I cry
out for aid, He ignores my prayer (v. 8; see Jer. 14:11–12).

The Lord is like some wild animal, a bear or a lion, lying in
wait for its prey. In such fashion He has dragged me off the
path and left me mangled and helpless (vv. 10–11). He is like
an enemy soldier or a skilled hunter who has drawn His bow
repeatedly to shoot the target, and *I* am that target. He has
pierced me through the heart (literally, kidneys) with arrows
from His quiver (vv. 12–13).

He has seen to it that my only food is bitter herbs, gall
(literally, wormwood; see v. 5), and gravel; He has trampled
me in the dust (vv. 15–16). He has deprived me of any peace
and certainly of any prosperity (in the sense of happiness;
v. 17). I am nothing more than a laughingstock to all my
people. They sing songs that mock me (see Jer. 20:7), and
they do so all day long (v. 14; see v. 3). (Perhaps they did so
because they considered him to be a guilty sinner being punished by the Lord.)

No wonder the poet concludes the section by lamenting
that his glory or strength is gone, along with all he had hoped
for from the Lord (v. 18).

B. A Personal Expression of Hope (3:19–39)

This is a passage of confidence, all the more precious and
important because it is so rare in this book. The clouds of
gloom are still present (vv. 19–20), but hope (see v. 18) in the
Lord's mercy cannot help but shine through. In this section
the poet takes a deeper, longer look and realizes that suffering
does not mean we are forsaken.

Yes, there is affliction and wandering. Yes, there is bitterness and gall (literally, wormwood, v. 19; see vv. 5, 15). They cannot be forgotten (v. 20). However, there is also the fact of God's love (v. 22; the great Heb. term *chesed*, covenant love or loyal love, Hos. 6:6–7). He affirms: I call to mind this reality and therefore I have hope.

It is only because of the Lord's great love that we are able to continue at all. Only because of Him are we not completely consumed. His compassions never fail. They are new every morning. They are so dependable because His faithfulness is great (vv. 22–23).

When my suffering was at its worst, I realized that my only true portion was in the Lord (see Num. 18:20). I can do nothing better and in fact nothing else than wait for Him (v. 24).

Verse 25 moves upward and outward in a crescendo of growing faith. The Lord is good. He is good to those who hope in Him. He is good to everyone who seeks Him. This is why it is good to wait eagerly for the deliverance (salvation) that is His alone and can come only from Him (v. 26).

Then the poet sinks back into his despair. He meditates on the reality of God's love and care; however, he can never escape the reality of the tragedy all around him. He speaks of bearing the yoke while one is young and able to do so (v. 27). He mentions sitting alone in silence because of all the Lord has laid on him (v. 28). He speaks of burying one's face in the dust (v. 29), perhaps in abject submission. The cheek may be exposed to the one who would strike it in an insulting way (v. 30; see Mic. 5:1).

Yet even then there may be hope (v. 29). The Lord does not cast us off forever. He brings grief, yes, but He also shows compassion because of His great and unfailing love (*chesed* again; vv. 30–32).

Then the author reaches one of the high points in his understanding of the Lord and of the tragedy of Judah's fall: The Lord does not bring affliction on us because He wants to. He does not choose to do so, and He certainly does not take delight in doing so. No, He causes grief to the children of men (mankind; v. 33) because He has to. Our rebellion leaves Him no other choice.

The Lord is the Most High (vv. 35, 38), in contrast to mere man (vv. 27, 35, 39). He will not allow evil to have the last word. Yes, He may have to crush underfoot all the prisoners of the land (of Palestine?). He may seem to deny people their rights. All the while, of course, He is well aware of what is going on (vv. 34–36). It obviously happens because He permits it to happen. He supervises the coming of both ill fortune (see Amos 3:6) and good (vv. 37–38; see Isa. 45:7). In the light of all this, why should any person complain because he is being punished for his sins? (v. 39).

The poet seems to have been growing both in confidence and in understanding. No wonder this passage reminds many people of Job 13:15: "Though he slay me, yet will I hope in him."

C. A Personal Expression of Repentance (3:40–58)

In the light of the confidence expressed above, it is time for the people to examine their ways. Verse 40 is the beginning of an appeal to the people to test their ways and return to the Lord. Lift up both hearts and hands in prayer, the poet urges (vv. 40–41). He even suggests a possible prayer for the repentant people to pray: "We have sinned and rebelled" (v. 42).

They have sinned, but the Lord has not forgiven them (v. 42). Instead, He has pursued after them in His intense anger. He has slain them without pity. He has turned their splendor (see v. 18) into nothing more than scum and refuse among the nations (vv. 43–45).

Because of the Lord's punishment the enemies have been able to open their mouths wide against the offenders (see 2:16). They have had to suffer terror, pitfalls, and ruin. Grief has come because of the plight of the women of the city. Streams of tears have flown because of the people's destruction (vv. 46–48, 51; see 1:16; Jer. 9:1).

But other tears should also flow—tears of penitence. They will flow continually until the day comes when the Lord will look down from heaven and see (vv. 49–50; see 1:9, 11, 20).

It is fascinating to study the relationship between punishment and repentance in these verses. It is because the enemies pursued him like hunters after a game bird that the poet calls on the Lord's name. They tried to kill him by throwing him into a pit and stoning him. The waters of death closed in over his head until he was sure he was about to be cut off (vv. 52–54).

But it was out of the depths of the pit of difficulty that he called on the Lord's name (v. 55). And in the context of this often depressing book, verse 56 virtually shouts in exaltation: "You heard my plea"! The pleas before this one were usually to the Lord to see or look (1:9, 11, 20; 3:50). In this case it is a plea to the Lord to hear: Hear my cry for relief. The most precious verses in the book so far must be verses 57–58:

> You came near when I called you,
> and you said, "Do not fear."
> O Lord, you took up my case;
> you redeemed my life.

Prayer was answered. Life was redeemed (by the *go'el*, the kinsman redeemer). And the prayer was answered with one of the truly great assurances in all of Scripture: "Do not fear."

D. A Personal Cry for Vengeance (3:59–66)

Lord, You have seen what I have gone through. You have seen all that has been done to me. You are aware of the depths of my enemies' vindictiveness toward me and all their plots against me. You have heard their malicious insults. Why, they whisper and mutter against me all day long. Look at them there. Whether they are sitting down or standing up, they never stop mocking me with their songs (vv. 60–63).

Lord, don't forsake me. And certainly don't ignore me. Uphold my cause. In fact, go further than that. Settle my account with my enemies. Pay them back what they deserve (see Ps. 28:4). Pay them back for what they have done (vv. 59, 64).

This is a typical Old Testament passage of imprecation. It is a prayer to the Lord, calling for a curse on the head of the enemy. So in verse 65 the poet asks the Lord to make their hearts dull by putting a veil over them. Pursue them in anger, he says. Destroy them as they have destroyed us. In fact, wipe them out from under the heavens (v. 66).

For Further Study

1. Think of the darkest time you have ever known. Rewrite 3:21–26 in your own words to express your personal confidence even in a time of difficulty.

2. In a theological wordbook look up the meaning of and various uses of the significant Hebrew term *chesed*.

3. Use a Bible dictionary or encyclopedia to make a study of the concept of kinsman-redeemer (Hebrew *go'el*) and the general Old Testament idea of redemption.

4. Use a Bible dictionary or encyclopedia, or an introduction to the Psalms, to study the idea of imprecation in the Old Testament.

Poem Four

From the Very Depths

Poem Four

From the Very Depths

(Lamentations 4:1-22)

This fourth poem is also an acrostic in the pattern we saw in chapters 1 and 2. It is unlike them in that the stanzas consist of two lines instead of three. As in the case of poem two, the sixteenth and seventeenth letters of the Hebrew alphabet are reversed. No one has ever been able to give a satisfactory explanation of this fact.

Once again we see the evident hand of an eyewitness who was able to describe the siege in the most vivid way.

A. The Horrors of the Siege (4:1-10)

In this third dirge, which again opens with "How" (see 1:1; 2:1), we have the sharp contrast between the before and the after. The gold has lost its luster. Even the brightest gold has become dull. The precious stones associated with the temple and its worship lie scattered around in the streets (v. 1) among the rubble. The stricken city and its people are like that, too (see v. 2).

Yes, things have changed. They have changed drastically. The precious people of Zion, who were considered so valuable, have sunk in worth down to the equivalent of a clay pot fashioned by the hand of a potter (v. 2). Most shards of pottery are not worth a dime a dozen in some of the more productive tels (ruins) in Palestine. They are thrown out by the basketfuls, perhaps to serve as gravel for a walkway, so that the more valuable pieces might be preserved. The poet says that the once-exalted people have become like that. Did those very people think of themselves as high-quality gold? Do we?

The poet uses two animal figures in verse 3. The first one pays grudging tribute to the parental instincts of a creature so often deprecated, the jackal. The other refers to a commonly held belief about the life pattern of the ostrich. The poet marvels at the contrast. Even the lowly mother jackal nurses her young during their infancy. The ostrich, however, had the reputation for being indifferent to the needs of its young (see Job 39:13–17). The first figure gives a contrast with the conduct of Jerusalem's people, the latter one an apt illustration.

Evidently the writer is implying here that the mothers of Judah have no other choice. The nursing mothers are themselves so deprived of food that they are unable to provide for their young. The result is the same as if they had no care at all for them. Thirst causes their babies' tongues to stick to the roofs of their mouths. Children beg for bread but nobody gives them anything to eat (v. 4), because there is nothing to give.

Even the fortunes of the rich have been reversed. Even they are going hungry, something that never happens when society is functioning normally. The poet points out that the ones who once ate only the richest of food are also destitute in the streets, as stricken as the needy have ever been. They may have worn purple in the past, as they lived in the lap of luxury, but they too now inhabit the trash heaps.

Such an overthrow strikes the poet as being more dramatic than that of the wicked city of Sodom, even though it was overthrown suddenly and quickly, without any hope of help.[1] In like fashion the princes of this little nation once had that well-fed glow of health. They shone among their fellows like snow or milk, like rubies (or coral) or lapis lazuli (see NIV mg.). But they have become gaunt, undernourished, and dehydrated. They are little more than skin and bones. They have become unrecognizable, blacker than soot. Their skin has shriveled; it looks like the bark of a dry stick (vv. 6–8; see 3:4). At least in the case of Sodom the punishment was over in a hurry.

Verse 9 is one of those rare but well-known Old Testament

---

[1]The last phrase of verse 6 may refer to the unexpected nature of the destruction, see NEB.

references that speak of death being preferable to life. It would have been better for someone to die by the sword than to have to starve to death. It would be better to die quickly than to linger, hungry, and to slowly waste away.

Verse 10 is one of the most gruesome verses in all of Scripture. However, we know that it accurately reflects the horrible conditions during the siege of Jerusalem. Mothers who really did care about their families had to cook their own children for food (see 2:20; Jer. 19:9). Evidently they had given up one of their children in order that others might be spared.

B. Reasons for the Horrors (4:11–16)

Once again comes the recognition that the Lord brought about all the tragedies that have come. He has given full vent to His wrath. He has fully poured out His fierce anger. He has set Zion afire with a flame of judgment that burned her down to her very foundations (v. 11). His anger against sin is a hot, hot fire.

But one reason such destruction has come from the Lord is that the people have been so overconfident. Nobody believed Jerusalem could be taken. The people did not believe it could be, and perhaps they had convinced themselves that others agreed (v. 12). The city had been built in a strategic military position. It had been extensively fortified and fiercely defended. However, no fortress stands when the Lord decrees that it will fall.

Another reason the nation fell was the sins of her religious leaders. Both prophets and priests were guilty. They not only failed to warn the people about their sins (2:14), they also joined the general and widespread oppression of the righteous poor (v. 13). They should have been holding up before the people the standards of the Lord's covenant; instead they were leading the pack in sin.

What a change has come in their status! Now they grope through the streets as if they are blind. They are so defiled with the blood of the innocent (see v. 13) that they are unclean; everyone treats them accordingly. People run them off as they might a leper who wanders into a normal social setting. All that is left is for them to flee the company of others

and wander about continually among the peoples of the nations because no one will let them remain (vv. 14–15).

As always, the Lord is credited with Judah's tragedy, as we
see in verse 16: the Lord Himself (literally, the face of
Yahweh) has scattered these guilty leaders. From those who
were supposedly His people He has withdrawn His watchful
care. As a consequence, life, both social and religious, is dis-
rupted: both elders and priests are no longer held in their
accustomed regard.

C. Just Recompense for All (4:17–22)

The final verses of the poem begin with a virtual reprise, a
recapping of the horrors of the destruction already so fully
described. The people looked so intently for the help that
never came that their eyes failed. They watched from the city
towers for the "friends" to come to their aid, but the watch
was in vain (v. 17).

During the final siege of Jerusalem by Nebuchadnezzar in
587 B.C., King Zedekiah appealed for help from the Egyptians.
They pretended to give it and sent an army in response to the
king's desperate appeal, as recorded in Jeremiah 37:5. The
Babylonians lifted the siege only long enough to send the
Egyptians scampering back to safety. This series of events
may well lie behind these verses.

Notice how the poet identifies himself with those who had
strained their eyes looking to Egypt for help that never mate-
rialized. Jeremiah never adopted such a position. He always
knew the hope for help was vain.

Trying to escape from the pursuers was also vain. The
people were hunted down by the enemy, who turned out to
be swifter than eagles. They chased any escapees over rugged
territory and ambushed them in waste places. It was even
unsafe to walk the streets of the city during the long siege.
Eventually everyone realized that Jeremiah had been right:
Jerusalem would fall. In fact, it was just a matter of time until
the end came (vv. 18–19).

Verse 19 may refer to King Zedekiah's short-lived escape
from the doomed city. Verse 20 almost certainly speaks of
him: "The LORD's anointed, our very life breath." He and a

few others were able to get as far as the Jordan Valley to the east, but the Babylonian conquerors caught them as if in a trap (2 Kings 25:4–7). The king was considered untouchable—he had divine protection. But with Zedekiah's capture died any hope Judah had of indigenous leadership or continued existence as a nation.

The poem ends with a brief but classic taunt song against Edom as representative of all of Judah's enemies (see Ps. 137:7). Notice the obvious verbal irony in verse 21, where the speaker says the opposite of what he means: "Oh, yes, Daughter of Edom, you go ahead and rejoice and be glad. You are just about to get yours." It is almost an "Enjoy yourself, it's later than you think" type of passage. You will have to drink the bitter cup of judgment, too. In fact, you will become drunk on it, and be exposed and shamed.

These descendants of Esau had apparently refused to join Judah and Egypt in rebellion against Babylon. They also helped the maurading armies in the closing days of the campaign and participated in the sacking of the city. After he took Jerusalem, Nebuchadnezzar gave Edom some of the southern rural areas of Judah as a reward. Such prosperity will vanish, the poet predicts.

So the poem ends on a wry note of hope. The most hated of enemies will suffer by having her wickedness exposed and her sin punished. The Daughter of Zion, on the other hand, will see her punishment end (v. 22). She will not have to face exile again. Truly there are going to be some changes made.

For Futher Study

1. What extreme conditions would be necessary to cause the mothers of Jerusalem to treat their children as described in this book?

2. Use a concordance to look up all of the Old Testament references to Sodom.

3. Under what circumstances would death ever be preferable to life (see 4:9), or one type of death preferable to another?

4. Locate Edom on a Bible map of this period. Then read about Edom in a Bible dictionary or encyclopedia.

Poem Five

From Misery a Prayer

Poem Five

From Misery a Prayer

(Lamentations 5:1-22)

The concluding dirge is notable, first of all, because it is the only poem in the book that is not an acrostic. The influence of the previous pattern continues, however, in that this poem, too, has twenty-two verses. Each verse consists of two lines that are matched in rhythm and also in content.

This poem emphasizes confession of sin and the Lord's sovereignty, themes already encountered throughout the book. It might be called more of a prayer than a lament. Perhaps we should call it a community confession instead of a community lament. The Latin Vulgate calls it a prayer of the prophet Jeremiah.

A. The Condition of Misery (5:1-18)

The prayer-character of the chapter becomes apparent from the first words: "Remember, O LORD, . . . look, and see," words common in Old Testament prayers (Exod. 32:13; Pss. 25:6; 74:2) and also in this book (1:9, 11, 20). The poet is insistent that the Lord be aware of what has happened to them, and the disgrace that is a part of it. Lord, please consider the terrible affliction of Your people.

The fact that such earnest prayer would be directed to the Lord under such difficult circumstances testifies to the poet's faith. His faith has been tested in the extreme, but it did not break.

The land You gave to Your people ("Our inheritance," v. 2; Lev. 20:24; Deut. 4:21) has become the possession of foreigners. Even our homes have fallen into the hands of foreigners. Those who are supposed to be the Lord's people have been turned out of land and home like orphans (v. 3).

We recall that after Jerusalem's fall in 587 B.C. the Edomites began to edge up into lower Judah, to eventually settle in the territory south of Hebron. Some Arab groups joined them in this occupation. The Lord had promised the land to the Hebrew people—in fact, it could have been theirs forever—but they forfeited their claim by their flagrant disobedience (see Deut. 4:25–27; Jer. 18:9–10). The land, you see, belonged not to Israel but to the Lord. They were allowed to live on it as tenants as long as they were faithful (Lev. 25:23).

The people now have become like those destitute of family. The conquering Chaldeans have so restricted and regulated their lives that they have to purchase the water of their own land to drink, as well as the wood for repairs and fuel (vv. 3–4).

Their conquerors were pursuers who never seem to tire and never let up. The defeated people of Judah, on the other hand, are bone-weary and unable to find rest (v. 5). The last line of verse 5 literally says "We are pursued to our very necks." This may refer to the ancient custom of the victor placing his foot on the neck of the defeated enemy, thus humiliating him and symbolizing his complete subjection (see Josh. 10:24). Others say the reference to the neck is an indication that the people had been reduced to slavery.

There is another reference in verse 6 to futile attempts to receive aid from foreign powers. Or perhaps the naming of the nations to the west and the east may indicate that the refugees might have to flee far from Palestine.[1] The mention of bread again indicates the shortage of food during the siege of the city.

Verse 7 is another of those verses in this little book so significant for the theology of the Exile. It reminds us of Ezekiel's quotation of the people's popular proverb about the fathers eating sour grapes but the children's teeth being set on edge (Ezek. 18:2). "Our fathers sinned," the people of Judah whine. They sinned to the extent that they were swept away in judgment. "And we bear their punishment."

---

[1]At this time Assyria was a vassal of Babylon.

It is always true that we are affected by the sins of other people (and vice versa), especially close family members. However, the Lord never holds us guilty or responsible for someone else's sin. In addition, the people of Judah seem to be implying that they themselves are innocent, and that the whole of the blame for their troubles rests with the older generation. Later (see v. 16) the poet acknowledges that his generation, too, bears a major responsibility.

It must be a terrible thing to be a slave of someone else—of anyone else. How much worse, however, and how much more degrading, to be the slave of a slave (v. 8). Not only do slaves rule over them; there is no prospect of liberation.

The slaves of verse 8 may mean Babylonian military officials charged with supervising the occupation of Judah (see 2 Kings 25:24). Perhaps by calling these officials "slaves" the poet is directing scorn at them. At any rate, the reference does serve to reinforce the people's dreadful condition.

These slaves of slaves are able to get something to eat only if they are willing to put their lives at risk (there was the constant danger of marauding bands of Bedouins who attacked the virtually defenseless villagers who might wander outside the settlements). As a result of the hunger and the terror, they are feverish with weakness and disease (vv. 9–10).

The innocent are often those who suffer the most in wartime. Women and girls must have suffered unthinkable indignities. Honored leaders have been dishonored in capture or perhaps even in death, one of the worst forms of insult among the Hebrews (vv. 11–12).

The list of those who suffer continues in the next two verses: the young are forced to engage in labor too heavy for them. The elders, who served as leaders of the community, no longer sit for deliberations on the low benches provided for them just inside the city gate. The young men have ceased to play and sing, because there is no longer anything to be happy or make music about (vv. 13–14).

Yes, their joy is gone. Mourning has replaced the celebration of dancing. Significantly, the section concludes with: "The crown has fallen from our head. Woe to us, for we have sinned" (v. 16). The "crown" seems to be a reference to the glory of a proud people, or perhaps their dignity and prestige. The Lord has rejected them, simply because they have first rejected Him.

Consequently the poet speaks for those whose hearts are weak and eyes dim. Mount Zion is a deserted ruin, so desolate that jackals prowl over it (vv. 17-18).

B. The Final Word: Prayer for Restoration (5:19-22)

The poem is desolate and depressing, but it does end on a more hopeful note. It ends with an earnest prayer to the Lord: Lord, may You reign forever. Your throne endures from generation to generation (which is a typical Hebrew way of saying "forever," see Pss. 93:2; 103:19).

Verse 20 is sharp in tone: Why do You keep on forgetting us? Why have You forsaken us for so long? The expression of confidence and trust in verse 19 has moved quickly into an implied cry of need: How can it be? This is not a question of doubt but of perplexity.

In verse 21 the prayer really gets down to business. No more timid leading up to the main point: Lord, restore us. "Restore us to yourself." Return us to Your side; renew us to what we were in the good old days.

Verse 21 is a wonderful, hopeful verse. It has always bothered some people that it is followed by verse 22, so that the book ends on a negative note (see also Isa. 66:24; Mal. 4:6). The Jewish people solved this problem by repeating verse 21 after verse 22 in their public synagogue readings.

You haven't rejected us completely, have you? You haven't utterly given up on us, haven't been so angry with us that there can never be any change, have You? (v. 22). Surely not. Surely, Lord, You will hear and answer our prayer to restore us to Yourself.

For Further Study

1. Write summary paragraphs on the view of Lamentations on the subjects of God, sin, and judgment.

2. Prepare a sermon, lesson, or devotional based on the Book of Lamentations, or write a song or contemporary poem expressing the feelings of the book.

Bibliography

Commentaries on Lamentations

Gottwald, Norman K. *Studies in the Book of Lamentations.* London: SCM Press, 1954.

Harrison, R. K. *Jeremiah and Lamentations: Introduction and Commentary.* Tyndale Old Testament Commentaries. Downers Grove, Illinois: Inter-Varsity Press, 1973.

Hillers, Dilbert R. *The Anchor Bible: Lamentations.* Garden City, New York: Doubleday and Company, Inc., 1972.

Kuist, Howard Tillman. *The Book of Jeremiah; The Lamentations of Jeremiah.* The Layman's Bible Commentary. Richmond, Virginia: John Knox Press, 1960.

Laurin, Robert B. *Lamentations.* The Broadman Bible Commentary. Nashville: Broadman Press, 1971.

Meek, Theophile J. *The Book of Lamentations.* The Interpreter's Bible. Nashville: Abingdon Press, 1956.

One Volume Commentaries

Dummelow, J. R., ed. *A Commentary on the Holy Bible.* New York: The Macmillan Company, 1952.

Laymon, Charles M., ed. *The Interpreter's One Volume Commentary on the Bible.* Nashville: Abingdon Press, 1971.

Introductions

Anderson, George W. *A Critical Introduction to the Old Testament.* London: Gerald Duckworth and Co. Ltd., 1959.

Childs, Brevard S. *Introduction to the Old Testament as Scripture.* Philadelphia: Fortress Press, 1979.

Driver, S. R. *An Introduction to the Literature of the Old Testament.* 9th ed. Edinburgh: T. & T. Clark, 1913.

Harrison, Ronald Kenneth. *Introduction to the Old Testament.* Grand Rapids: Wm. B. Eerdmans Publishing Company, 1969.

Bible Dictionaries and Encyclopedias

Buttrick, George Arthur, ed. *The Interpreter's Dictionary of the Bible.* 4 vols. Nashville: Abingdon Press, 1982.

Douglas, J. D., ed. *The New Bible Dictionary.* Wheaton, Illinois: Tyndale House Publishers, Inc., 1982.

Tenney, Merrill C., ed. *The Zondervan Pictorial Encyclopedia of the Bible.* 5 vols. Grand Rapids: Zondervan Publishing House, 1975.